GOAT MOVES OUT of the BARNYARD

T0084478

by Nikki Potts • illustrated by Maarten Lenoir

PICTURE WINDOW BOOKS
a capstone imprint

Goat gets fed every
day at the farm.
There is plenty to eat.

It's good food.
But it's goat food.

Goat wonders what it would be like to try something new.

Hey, you! Ready for something new?

A tropical vacation sounds like a delicious place to start Goat's foodie adventure!

OUCH!
Pineapples are
pointy!

Coconuts
are too hard!
Not even Goat's
tough skull can
crack one.

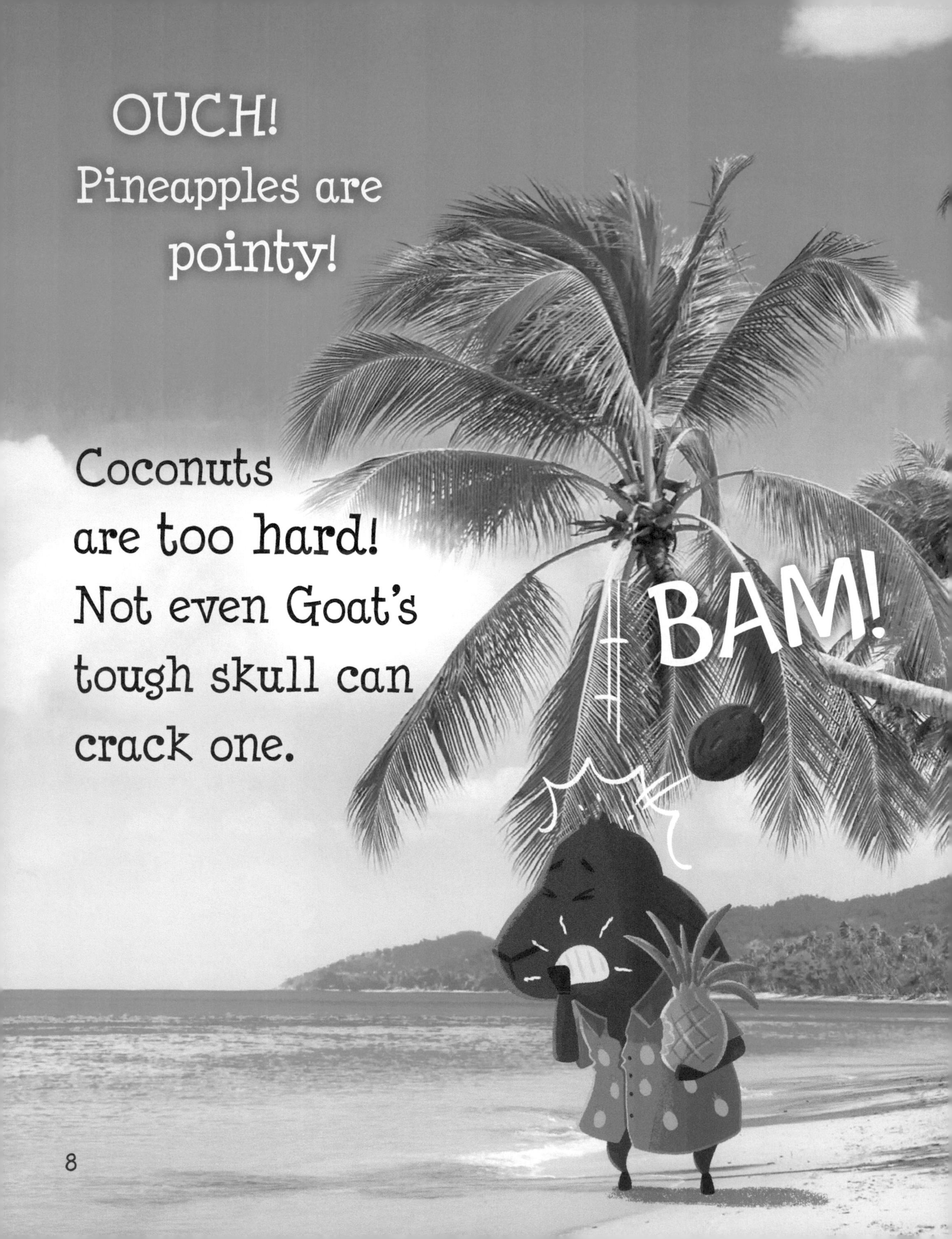

BAM!

And it's impossible to peel bananas without hands.

Goat gives up.

The wetlands have lots of yummy grasses.

They're crunchy and salty.

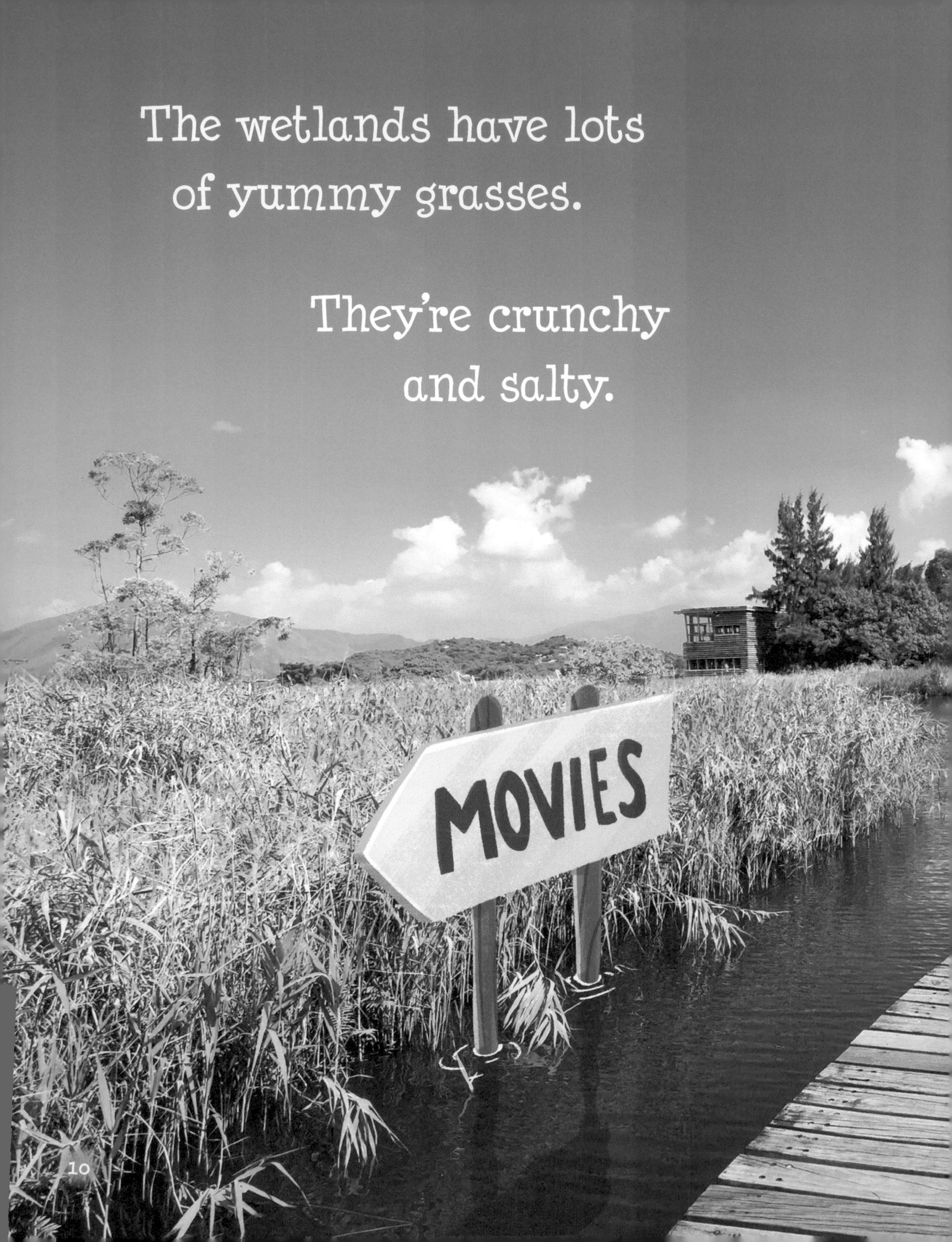

Goat might

like it here.

Still, something seems wrong.

Goat feels like he
is being watched.

The wetlands are much too scary for Goat.

YIKES!

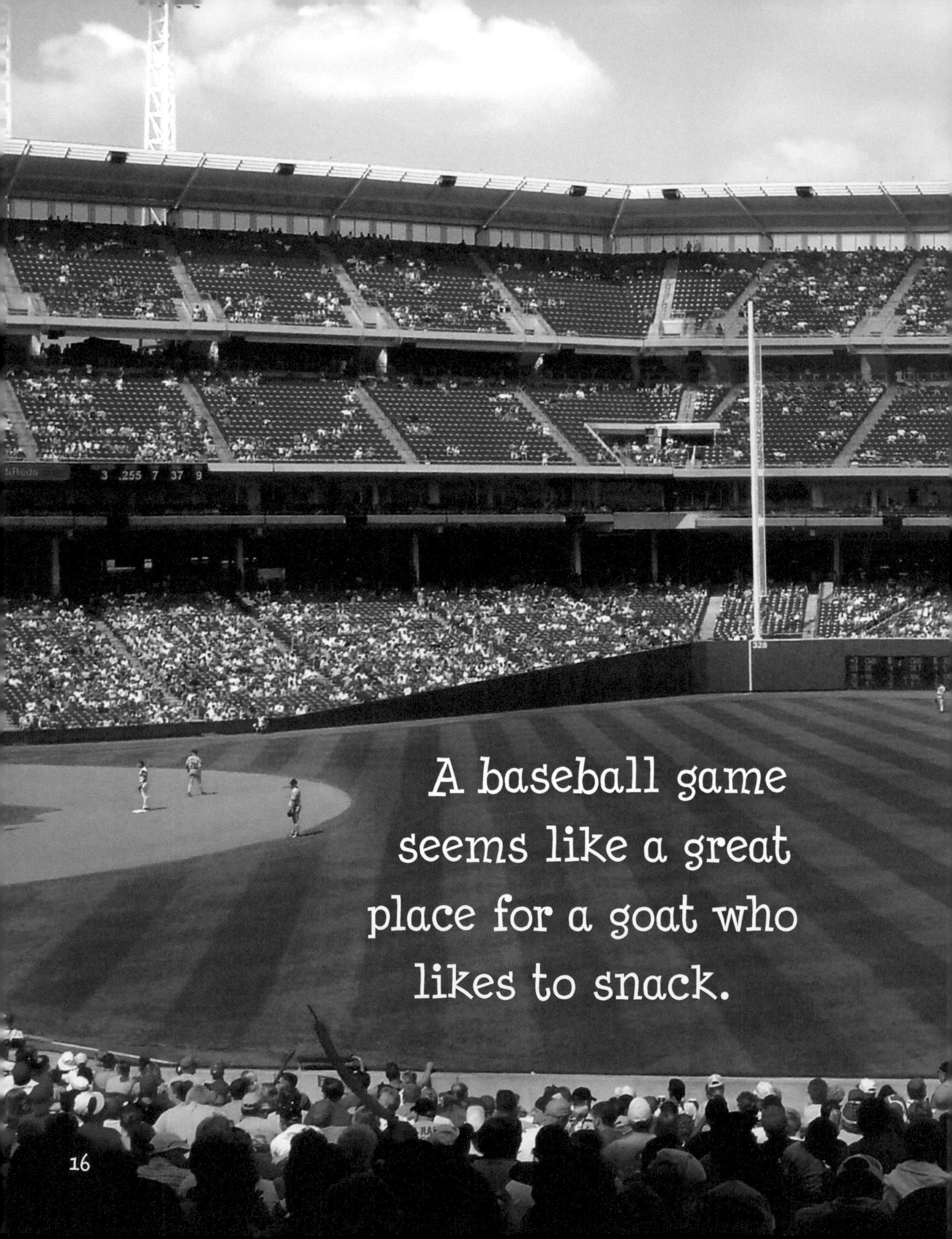

A baseball game seems like a great place for a goat who likes to snack.

9 .236 3 21 0
9 .236 3 21
379
G

There are plenty of choices for Goat to choose from. He loves peanuts, Cracker Jacks, and all the other game-day goodies!

G

WATCH OUT!

Goat does NOT love foul balls.

Goat's head hurts. He is also still hungry. He wants something sugary sweet to fill his grumbly stomach.

Goat is like a kid in a candy store.

Actually, Goat IS a kid in a candy store!

UGH.

Too.
Much.
Candy.

Goat has a bellyache!

The only thing that will make Goat feel better is some plain food.

Goat has missed his hay.
He missed his safe pasture.

The farm really is the
best home for Goat.

MORE ABOUT NIGERIAN DWARF GOATS

Nigerian dwarf goats are dairy goats. They produce milk.

These goats can be many colors including spotted, brown, black, gold, and other patterns.

Nigerian dwarf goats first came from West Africa. Today they can be found all over the world.

Some Nigerian dwarf goats have horns. They can also have beards.

Nigerian dwarf goats are very playful.

ANIMAL PASSPORT

Name: Nigerian Dwarf Goat

Type: goat/mammal

Habitat: farm

Diet: plants/hay

Height: 22 to 23 inches
(56 to 58 centimeters)

Weight: 30 to 45 pounds
(14 to 20 kilograms)

Lifespan: 12 to 14 years

Favorite Activity: jumping on the trampoline

BOOKS IN THIS SERIES

Habitat Hunter is published by Picture Window Books, an imprint of Capstone.
1710 Roe Crest Drive
North Mankato, Minnesota 56003
www.capstonepub.com

Copyright © 2020 by Capstone. All rights reserved. No part of this publication may be reproduced in whole or in part, or stored in a retrieval system, or transmitted in any form or by any means, electronic, mechanical, photocopying, recording, or otherwise, without written permission of the publisher.

Library of Congress Cataloging-in-Publication Data is available on the Library of Congress website.
ISBN: 978-1-9771-1421-1 (library binding)
ISBN: 978-1-9771-2019-9 (paperback)
ISBN: 978-1-9771-1427-3 (eBook PDF)

Summary: Goat is bored with its habitat! Follow Goat as it tries out different places to live. Which habitat will make the best home for Goat?

Image Credits
Shutterstock: coloursinmylife, 10-11, daizuoxin, 12-13, Dmytro Gilitukha, 22-23, 24-25, Dominique Saling, 28-29, Dudarev Mikhail, 5, happystock, 9, jaroslava V, 2-3, Kelly vanDellen, 21, ltummy, cover, Nick Fox, cover, Olesya Kuprina, 6-7, Paul Yates, 20, r.classen, 14-15, SS pixels, 26-27, Stockagogo by Barhorst, 16-17, SunflowerMomma, 31, Taylor Griffin, 18-19, Tom Gowanlock, 4-5, Vector8DIY, back cover, Vixit, 8

Artistic Elements: pingebat, Valeriya_Dor

Editorial Credits
Editor: Mari Bolte; Designer: Kayla Rossow; Media Researcher: Kelly Garvin; Production Specialist: Tori Abraham

All internet sites appearing in back matter were available and accurate when this book was sent to press.

Printed in the United States 5735